A VISIT TO

Colombia

REVISED AND UPDATED

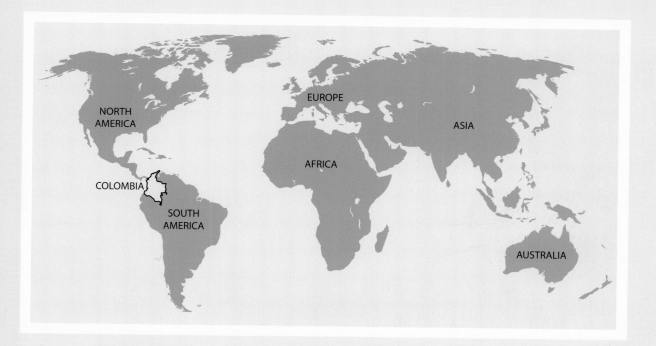

NORTH AMERICA

EUROPE

ASIA

AFRICA

COLOMBIA

SOUTH AMERICA

AUSTRALIA

Mary Virginia Fox

Heinemann Library
Chicago, Illinois

Customer Service 888-454-2279
Visit our website at www.heinemannraintree.com

Designed by Joanna Hinton-Malivoire
Printed in China by South China Printing Company Limited

13 12 11 10 09
10 9 8 7 6 5 4 3 2 1

New edition ISBN-10: 1-4329-1280-1(hardcover), 1-4329-1299-2 (paperback)
New edition ISBN-13: 978-1-4329-1280-2 (hardcover), 978-1-4329-1299-4 (paperback)

The Library of Congress has cataloged the first edition as follows:
Fox, Mary Virginia.
    Colombia / Mary Virginia Fox.
        p. cm. – (A visit to)
    Includes bibliographical references and index.
    Summary: An introduction to the land, culture, and people of Colombia.
    ISBN 1-57572-378-6 (library binding)
    1. Colombia—Juvenile literature. [1. Colombia.] I. Title. II. Series.

F2258.5 .F69 2000
986.1—dc21
                                                        00-029551

Acknowledgments
The publishers would like to thank the following for permission to reproduce photographs: © Aurora p. 21 (PictureQuest/Jose Azel); © Contact Press Images p. 6 (PictureQuest/Frank Fournier); © Corbis pp. 7 (Richard Bickel), 9 (Jeremy Horner), 11 (Richard Bickel), 15 (Jeremy Horner), 16 (Enzo and Paolo Ragazzini), 17 (Jeremy Horner), 18 (The Purcell Team), 19 (The Purcell Team), 20 (Ted Spiegel), 22 (Jeremy Horner), 24 (Jeremy Horner), 25 (Jeremy Horner), 26 (Jeremy Horner), 28 (Jeremy Horner), 29; © Eye Ubiquitous p. 10 (Corbis/Omar Bechara Baruque); © Getty Images (AFP Photo/ Luis Acosta) p. 27; © Jupiter/FoodPix pp. 12, 13; © Lonely Planet p. 14; © Photolibrary Group p. 8 (PhotoDisc/Medio Images [Jupiter]); © Photos.com [Jupiter] p. 5; © Victor Englebert p. 23.

Cover photograph reproduced with permission of © Lonely Planet (Krzysztof Dydynski).

Every effort has been made to contact copyright holders of any material reproduced in this book. Any omissions will be rectified in subsequent printings if notice is given to the publisher.

Contents

Any words appearing in bold, **like this**, are explained in the Glossary.

Colombia

Key
- Land above 0 ft/0 m/sea level
- Land above 1,000 ft/305 m
- Land above 10,000 ft/3,048 m
- Capital
- Important cities

Colombia is a large country in South America. It is almost as large as the state of Alaska.

Colombia is a beautiful country. It has rain forests and beaches. There are also ruins and important places from history there.

Colombia's **coasts** are nearly 2000 miles (3200 kilometers) long all together.

Land

In the mountains of Colombia it is very cold. In the jungles it is hot. Most people live somewhere in between.

Parts of Colombia are very different from one another. You can go to the beach and still see the tops of mountains that are miles away. There are also **plains** called *llanos*.

Part of the **coast** of Colombia is on the Pacific Ocean and part is on the **Caribbean Sea**.

Landmarks

The **capital** city is called Bogotá.
People come to visit the beautiful
cathedral and El Sagrario Chapel.
They are on a large **plaza**.

Cartagena was built nearly 500 years ago.

There is an old stone fort in a city called Cartagena. It was used to protect the city. The fort was attacked many times.

Homes

In the cities, most people live in apartments. There are large homes, too. You can also see modern steel and glass **skyscrapers**.

In the jungle, homes are built of **palm thatch** and wooden poles. In the country, some homes are built of clay or stone. Many have red tile roofs.

Homes in the country have palm trees and banana trees around them.

Food

Soups are an important part of a meal. They can be made of meat and vegetables, such as corn and potatoes. A favorite food is **arepa**, a tasty cornbread.

Everyone drinks coffee in Colombia.

Colombia is known all over the world for its coffee. Children and adults drink coffee. But children drink their coffee with milk.

Clothes

In the cities, most Colombians dress like people in big cities everywhere. They often wear bright colors. People dress in their very best clothes on Sundays.

In colder parts of the country, people wear shawls called **ruanas** and **felt** hats. In the hot, wet parts of Colombia, people usually wear shorts and T-shirts.

Work

Many people work in stores, offices, and factories. They make cars and furniture. They weave cloth and make clothing.

There are many small farms in the country. Families grow fruit, sugar, coffee, and vegetables. Some people herd cattle on the **plains**. Other people work in **emerald** mines.

Transportation

Outside the cities, few roads are paved. Most people use buses to get from one village to another. Some people ride mules or horses to get from place to place.

Colombia has more than 11 thousand miles (18 thousand kilometers) of waterways.

There are not many railroads because of the mountains in Colombia. On the rivers, boats carry people and **produce**. Airlines connect the main cities of Colombia with other countries.

Languages

Most people in Colombia speak Spanish. This is because Colombia was **settled** by people from Spain. Many people in the cities also understand and speak English.

Some people who live in the mountains or the **tropics** do not speak Spanish or English. They speak their own **native languages**.

School

Children go to school when they are five years old. They can leave school when they are 16. In some schools, children wear uniforms.

In the country, the school may not be inside a building. In some villages, a radio is set up in a public place. Families bring their children to hear the lessons on the radio.

Free Time

Many towns and villages have a place
where bullfights are held. Soccer and
baseball are also popular. There have
been some famous bicycle racers
from Colombia.

Music and dancing are part of most people's lives. Some people play instruments such as flutes or **gourds** filled with pebbles that rattle. There is a **folk dance** called **bambuco** that people still dance today.

Celebrations

Carnival is a special celebration. There are parades and music. Other **festivals** are for religious holidays. At one festival, people paint their faces black or white.

Soldiers stand guard with the Colombian flag on Independence Day.

People in Colombia celebrate Independence Day on July 20. It is a noisy day with fireworks and dancing in the streets.

The Arts

There were people who lived in Colombia long ago. They made huge statues of stone. They also made beautiful gold statues and jewelry.

Fernando Botero is a famous artist from Colombia. He is known for his colorful paintings of families. He also makes big statues.

Fact File

Name	The Republic of Colombia is the country's full name.
Capital	The **capital** city is called Bogotá.
Language	Most people speak Spanish.
Population	There are nearly 45 million people living in Colombia.
Money	Colombian money is called the peso.
Religions	Most people in Colombia belong to the Roman Catholic Church.
Products	Gold and **emeralds** are mined from the earth. Wood for furniture and paper comes from the forests. Coffee and sugarcane grow on large farms. Factory workers make refrigerators and other things for homes.

Words you can learn

adiós (ah-dee-OS)	goodbye
buenos días (BWAY-nohs DEE-yahs)	good morning
buenas noches (BWAY-nahs NOH-chez)	good night
gracias (GRAH-see-yahs)	thank you
de nada (day NAH-dah)	you're welcome
sí (see)	yes
uno/una (oonoh/oonah)	one
dos (dohs)	two
tres (trays)	three

Glossary

arepa type of cornbread that is popular in Colombia (You say ah-RAY-pah.)

bambuco traditional dance of Colombia (You say bahm-BOO-co.)

capital important city where the government is based

cathedral large, important church

coast land at the edge of an ocean

emerald valuable green stone used to make jewelry

felt heavy material made from wool

festival party held by a whole town or country

folk dance dance that people in a country have danced for a long time

gourd large fruit with a hard shell that can be dried to make cups, bowls, or musical instruments

llano Spanish word for a large, flat area of land covered in grass (You say YAH-noh.)

native language language that has been spoken in a place since before other people brought their own language

palm thatch very large leaves from a palm tree stacked up on top of each other to make a covering that keeps out rain

plain flat land covered in grass or small bushes

plaza public square in a city or town that has statues, gardens, or fountains

produce fresh food such as fruit and vegetables

ruana large, square shawl that is pulled on over the head (You say roo-AH-nah.)

settled moved from one country to live in another country

skyscraper tall building in a city

tropics place where the weather is very hot and wet

Index